LOMBOK TRAVEL GUIDE 2024: LATEST EXPLORATION TIPS

EMBARK ON NEW HORIZONS WITH DEFINITIVE INSIDER CLUES FOR BEST EXPLORATION

MICHELLE CLANT

Copyright © 2024 by Michelle Clant

All rights reserved.

No part of this publication may be reproduced, distributed, or transmitted in any form or by any means, including photocopying, recording, or other electronic or mechanical methods, without the prior written permission of the author, except in the case of brief quotations embodied in critical reviews and certain other noncommercial uses permitted by copyright law.

Aerial View of Lombok City

Table of Contents

Chapter One
Introduction to Lombok
- 1.1 Lombok's Enchanting Allure: Unveiling the Island's Unique Charm
- 1.2 Beyond Bali's Shadow: Discovering Lombok's Untamed Beauty
- 1.3 A Tapestry of Cultures: Exploring Lombok's Rich Heritage and Traditions
- 1.4 Navigating the Island: Essential Travel Tips and Getting Around

Chapter Two
Unveiling the Landscapes of Lombok
- 2.1 Majestic Mount Rinjani: Trekking to the Heart of Lombok's Volcanic Majesty
- 2.2 Emerald Jungles and Cascading Waterfalls: Immersing in Lombok's Natural Splendor
- 2.3 Pristine Beaches and Hidden Coves: Unwinding on Lombok's Idyllic Coastline
- 2.4 Beyond the Coast: Exploring Lombok's Enchanting Rice Terraces and Villages

Chapter Three
Cultural Delights of Lombok
- 3.1 The Rhythm of Sasak Traditions: Experiencing Lombok's Vibrant Art, Music, and Dance
- 3.2 Unveiling the Secrets of Wastra: Immerse in Lombok's Textile Weaving

Artisanship

3.3 A Culinary Adventure: Savoring the Authentic Flavors of Lombok Cuisine

3.4 Temple Tales: Discovering Lombok's Sacred Hindu and Islamic Heritage

Chapter Four

Adventures for Every Thrill Seeker

4.1 Surfing Paradise: Conquering Lombok's Epic Waves and Hidden Breaks

4.2 Diving into Coral Kingdoms: Exploring Lombok's Underwater World of Rich Biodiversity

4.3 Trekking through Time: Embarking on Historical Trails and Cultural Journeys

4.4 Beyond the Ordinary: Caving, Cycling, and Kayaking through Lombok's Diverse Terrain

Chapter Five

Unveiling Lombok's Gilis: Island Hopping Paradise

5.1 Gili Trawangan: A Buzzing Hive of Activity and Party Vibes

5.2 Gili Air: Tranquil Escape for Relaxation and Romance

5.3 Gili Meno: Honeymoon Haven and Snorkeling Sanctuary

5.4 Island Hopping Delights: Discovering the Untouched Charms of Smaller Gili Islands

Chapter Six

Lombok for Nature Lovers

6.1 Birdwatching Bonanza: Spotting Endemic Species in Lombok's National Parks

6.2 Jungle Encounters: Trekking through Lush Rainforests and Spotting Exotic Wildlife

6.3 Marine Marvels: Conservation Efforts and Protecting Lombok's Underwater Treasures

6.4 Sustainable Travel: Responsible Tourism Practices for a Greener Lombok

Chapter Seven

Family Fun in Lombok

7.1 Splashing Adventures: Water Parks, Beaches, and Family-Friendly Activities

7.2 Educational Escapades: Cultural Learning Experiences and Museums for Kids

7.3 Wildlife Encounters: Zoos, Animal Sanctuaries, and Responsible Wildlife Interactions

7.4 Family-Friendly Accommodation: Choosing the Perfect Resort for Fun and Relaxation

Chapter Eight

Lombok Beyond the Tourist Trail

8.1 Secret Beaches and Hidden Gems: Discovering Off-the-Beaten-Path Paradises

8.2 Local Markets and Authentic Experiences: Immerse in the Daily Life of Lombok's Villages

8.3 Homestays and Cultural Exchanges:

Staying with Locals and Experiencing True Lombok Hospitality

8.4 Volunteering Opportunities: Contributing to Conservation Efforts and Local Communities

Chapter Nine
Essential Information for Your Lombok Trip

9.1 Visa Requirements and Immigration Procedures

9.2 Currency Exchange and Money Matters

9.3 Transportation Options and Getting Around Lombok

9.4 Health and Safety Tips for a Safe and Healthy Journey

Chapter Ten
Memories that Last a Lifetime

10.1 Capturing the Essence of Lombok: Photography Tips and Souvenirs to Bring Home

10.2 Sharing Your Lombok Story: Travel Blogging and Social Media Inspiration

10.3 Responsible Tourism: Minimizing Your Footprint and Leaving a Positive Impact

10.4 Until We Meet Again: Saying Goodbye to Lombok and Planning Your Next Return

Chapter One

Introduction to Lombok

1.1 Lombok's Enchanting Allure: Unveiling the Island's Unique Charm

Lombok, the sister island of Bali, shimmers like a hidden gem in the Indonesian archipelago. While its neighbor often hogs the spotlight with its vibrant culture and established tourism scene, Lombok whispers a different kind of enchantment. Beyond the postcard-perfect beaches and dramatic volcanic peaks, a tapestry of unspoiled landscapes, rich traditions, and warm hospitality awaits. In Lombok, time dances to a slower rhythm, beckoning travelers to shed their routines and immerse themselves in the island's unique charm.

This is a land where turquoise waters lap against pristine shores, and emerald rice paddies paint the foothills of majestic Mount Rinjani. Lush rainforests whisper secrets in the breeze, while ancient villages hum with the sounds of daily life unchanged for centuries.

Lombok's charm lies not just in its breathtaking beauty, but in its authenticity. Here, traditional Sasak culture thrives, manifested in intricately woven textiles, mesmerizing music and dance, and a genuine embrace of visitors.

Unlike Bali, Lombok hasn't yet surrendered to the relentless march of mass tourism. It retains a sense of untamed wilderness, inviting adventurous spirits to explore hidden coves, trek through virgin jungles, and discover waterfalls cascading into secret pools. The pace is laid-back, the atmosphere unpretentious, and the smiles of the locals as warm as the tropical sun. Lombok is a canvas waiting to be painted, an island offering a chance to reconnect with nature, embrace cultural treasures, and create memories that linger long after you bid farewell.

1.2 Beyond Bali's Shadow: Discovering Lombok's Untamed Beauty

Often overshadowed by its glitzier neighbor, Lombok offers a refreshing alternative for those seeking an escape from the crowds and curated experiences. While Bali pulsates with energy and a kaleidoscope of offerings, Lombok whispers promises of tranquility and genuine cultural immersion. This doesn't mean Lombok lacks excitement. Its rugged terrain, dotted with volcanic peaks and verdant valleys, is a playground for outdoor enthusiasts. Hikers can conquer the slopes of Mount Rinjani, the second-highest volcano in Indonesia, while surfers chase epic waves along the island's pristine coastline. Divers marvel at the vibrant coral reefs teeming with marine life, while kayakers and paddleboarders weave through networks of mangrove forests and hidden coves.

Beyond the thrill of adventure, Lombok beckons with a cultural richness that surpasses the surface. Villages untouched by the tide of mass tourism offer glimpses into a way of life unchanged for generations. Witness the intricate craft of Sasak women weaving "ikat" textiles, a vibrant explosion of colors and patterns. Attend a traditional "Kecak" fire dance, where the hypnotic chanting of hundreds of men creates a trance-like atmosphere. Wander through bustling markets overflowing with exotic fruits, handcrafted souvenirs, and the infectious laughter of locals. Every corner of Lombok unveils a new facet of its vibrant tapestry, waiting to be unraveled by curious travelers.

Lombok's beauty lies not just in its landscapes and culture, but in its untouchedness. Here, beaches haven't been colonized by sun loungers, and the pace of life remains delightfully unhurried. It's an island where you can reconnect with nature's raw beauty, lose yourself in the rhythm of traditional life, and discover a slice of Indonesia unmarred by commercialization. So, step out of Bali's shadow and embark on a journey to Lombok, where authentic experiences and unspoiled beauty await at every turn.

1.3 Diverse Cultures: Exploring Lombok's Rich Heritage and Traditions

Lombok's cultural landscape is a vibrant tapestry woven from diverse threads. The dominant Sasak culture, with its strong animist roots, lays the foundation. Their belief in the interconnectedness of nature and spirits manifests in captivating rituals, mesmerizing music and dance, and a deep respect for the land. Witness the "Ngaben" ceremony, where a deceased soul's journey towards reincarnation is celebrated with colorful processions and offerings. In Lombok's villages, listen to the haunting melodies of the "gendang beleq" bamboo ensemble, or marvel at the rhythmic stomping of the "Rudat" dance, where stories of ancient battles unfold.

Lombok's history whispers amidst ancient Hindu temples and mosques reflecting the island's spiritual crossroads. Explore the majestic Mayura temple, a testament to Balinese influence, or wander through the serenity of Islamic shrines steeped in Arabic traditions. Each village holds its own unique customs and celebrations, from the boisterous "Bau Nyale" harvest festival, where thousands flock to the shores to collect sea worms, to the solemn "Lebaran" festivities marking the end of Ramadan.

Beyond the mainstays, Lombok offers glimpses into lesser-known cultural gems. Discover the fascinating "Wetu Telu" belief system, which blends elements of Islam, Hinduism, and animism, or witness the intricate art of woodcarving and silversmithing passed down through generations. Every interaction, every encounter, unveils another fragment of Lombok's rich cultural mosaic, leaving you enriched and intrigued.

1.4 Navigating the Island: Essential Travel Tips and Getting Around

Planning your Lombok adventure starts with essential knowledge. Visa requirements for most nationalities are straightforward, while currency exchange is readily available at airports and banks. Local transportation offers a range of options, from bustling public buses and colorful bemo vans to private taxis and motorbike rentals. For island hopping, ferries connect Lombok to the captivating Gili Islands, offering opportunities for diving, snorkeling, and exploring pristine beaches.

Embrace the laid-back pace of Lombok but be prepared for some logistical quirks. While English is understood in tourist areas, learning basic Bahasa Indonesia phrases goes a long way. ATMs are readily available, but cash comes in handy for smaller purchases and local markets. Pack for a tropical climate with comfortable clothing, sunscreen, and insect repellent. Respect local customs, especially when visiting religious sites, and dress modestly.

Accommodation options range from charming homestays in traditional villages to luxurious resorts nestled amidst breathtaking scenery. To delve deeper into the island's soul, consider staying in local communities, where authentic experiences and warm hospitality await. Embrace the unexpected, be flexible with plans, and allow yourself to be swept away by the island's unique rhythm.

1.5 Useful Phrases in Lombok

Basic Conversations:

Hello: Halo (hah-low)
Goodbye: Selamat jalan (seh-lah-mat jah-lan)
Thank you: Terima kasih (teh-ree-mah kah-sih)
You're welcome: Sama-sama (sah-mah sah-mah)
Excuse me: Permisi (peh-ree-mee-see)
Do you speak English?: Apakah kamu bisa berbahasa Inggris? (ah-pah kah-mu bi-sah ber-bah-sah ahng-gris)
I don't understand: Saya tidak mengerti (sah-yah tee-dak men-ger-tee)
How much is this?: Berapa ini? (beh-rah-pah ee-nee)
Can I have the bill, please?: Boleh minta billnya? (boh-leh min-ta bill-nyah)

Greetings:

Good morning: Selamat pagi (seh-lah-mat pah-gi)
Good afternoon: Selamat siang (seh-lah-mat see-ang)
Good evening: Selamat malam (seh-lah-mat mah-lam)
How are you?: Apa kabar? (ah-pah kah-bar)
I'm fine, thank you: Baik, terima kasih (baik, teh-ree-mah kah-sih)

Ordering Food:

Can I have this, please?: Boleh saya pesan ini? (boh-leh sah-yah peh-san ee-nee)
One, please: Satu, tolong (sah-too, toh-long)
Can I have the check, please?: Boleh minta billnya? (boh-leh min-ta bill-nyah)
This is delicious: Ini enak sekali (ee-nee eh-nak seh-kah-lee)

Numbers 1-10:

Satu (sah-too)
Dua (doo-ah)
Tiga (tee-gah)
Empat (em-pat)
Lima (lee-mah)

Enam (eh-nam)
Tujuh (too-juh)
Delapan (deh-lah-pan)
Sembilan (seh-mbee-lan)
Sepuluh (seh-poo-loo)

Directions:

Where is...? Di mana...? (dee mah-nah...)
Can you show me the way to...? Bisakah Anda menunjukkan jalan ke...? (bee-sah-kah ah-nda me-nun-jook-kan jah-lan keh...)
Go straight: Lurus (loo-roos)
Turn left: Belok kiri (beh-lok kee-ree)
Turn right: Belok kanan (beh-lok kah-nan)
Stop: Berhenti (ber-hen-tee)

Additional Tips:

Smile and make eye contact when speaking. Speak slowly and clearly.

Don't be afraid to make mistakes; most locals appreciate the effort to speak their language. There are many regional dialects of Bahasa Indonesia, so some pronunciation may vary.
I hope these phrases and tips help you navigate your conversations and interactions in Lombok! Have a wonderful trip!

Chapter Two
Unveiling the Landscapes of Lombok

2.1 Majestic Mount Rinjani: Trekking to the Heart of Lombok's Volcanic Majesty

Towering over the island like a watchful giant, Mount Rinjani is the beating heart of Lombok's landscape. This active volcano, the second-highest in Indonesia, ignites the adventurous spirit with its promise of breathtaking panoramas and challenging climbs. Trekking through its diverse terrain is an experience etched in memory, a journey that unveils the raw beauty and untamed wilderness of Lombok.

Rinjani's slopes offer trails for every level, from seasoned veterans tackling the demanding ascent to the summit crater lake to leisurely walks amidst verdant foothills. Whether you choose a multi-day adventure or a scenic day hike, the rewards are immense. Witness the sun painting the sky in fiery hues as it rises above the clouds, gaze into the turquoise depths of Segara Anak crater lake, and feel the exhilaration of conquering every switchback of the rugged climb.

Beyond the physical challenge, Rinjani's magic lies in its diverse ecosystems. Trek through lush rainforests teeming with exotic flora and fauna, pass by shimmering waterfalls cascading down moss-covered rocks, and breathe in the invigorating air scented with volcanic minerals. Encounter local communities living in harmony with the mountain, their traditional houses blending seamlessly with the landscape. Each step reveals a new vista, a hidden wonder, leaving you awestruck by the sheer power and beauty of nature.

Climbing Rinjani requires preparation and respect for the mountain's unpredictable nature. Choose reputable guides, pack essential gear, and prioritize your safety. But more importantly, surrender to the rhythm of the ascent, embrace the camaraderie of fellow trekkers, and savor the awe-inspiring moments that await at every turn. Remember, reaching the summit isn't just a physical goal; it's a transformative journey that will leave you humbled, rejuvenated, and forever connected to the spirit of Lombok.

2.2 Emerald Jungles and Cascading Waterfalls: Immersing in Lombok's Natural Splendor

Step beyond the sun-kissed beaches and venture into the verdant heart of Lombok, where emerald jungles whisper secrets and cascading waterfalls sing their siren song. These lush rainforests, cloaked in mist and vibrant with life, offer a sanctuary for weary souls and adventurous spirits. Embark on jungle trails dappled with sunlight, breathe in the fresh scent of damp earth and exotic flowers, and lose yourself in the symphony of rustling leaves and chirping birds.

Lombok's hidden waterfalls are like glistening jewels scattered across the landscape. Trek through dense foliage to unveil secret cascades plunging into crystal-clear pools, hidden from the outside world. Take a refreshing dip in the cool water, listen to the rhythmic gush of the fall, and let the natural mist revitalize your senses. Hike alongside cascading streams, witness rainbows dancing in the spray, and discover hidden grottoes beneath the cascading veil. These waterfalls are not just scenic wonders; they are portals to tranquility, inviting you to reconnect with nature's raw power and beauty.

Beyond the jungles and waterfalls, Lombok's natural splendor unfolds in diverse landscapes. Explore serene rice terraces carved into hillsides, their emerald hues reflecting the sky. Trek through rugged canyons carved by ancient rivers, marveling at the towering rock formations and vibrant birds soaring overhead. Discover hidden hot springs bubbling with geothermal energy, offering a chance to soak in the island's natural rejuvenation. Whether you seek adrenaline-pumping adventures or serene moments of quietude, Lombok's natural landscapes hold a treasure for every seeker.

2.3 Pristine Beaches and Hidden Coves: Unwinding on Lombok's Idyllic Coastline

Lombok's coastline stretches like a jewel-studded necklace around the island, offering a paradise for sun-seekers, surfers, and beach lovers alike. Turquoise waters lap against pristine sands, fringed by swaying palm trees and dramatic cliffs. Forget crowded resorts and bustling scenes; Lombok's beaches whisper promises of secluded coves, hidden gems waiting to be discovered.

Indulge in the ultimate beach holiday experience on stretches like Selong Beach, where soft sand stretches for miles, inviting long walks and leisurely dips. For those seeking solitude, secluded bays like Tanjung Aan and Mawun offer intimate havens, where the sounds of crashing waves and chirping birds are the only companions. Embrace the thrill of surfing world-class breaks like Gerupuk and Desert Point, where epic waves challenge seasoned surfers and mesmerize onlookers.

Beyond the famous hotspots, Lombok's coastline is dotted with secret coves accessible only by foot or local boat. Hike through rugged coastal paths, kayak through mangrove forests, or rent a local fishing boat to unveil hidden oases. Discover secluded havens like Tiu Kelep Island, a sanctuary of tranquility and turquoise waters, or Sekotong Island, where colorful fishing villages and coral reefs teeming with life await.

Lombok's beaches offer more than just sun and sand. Witness the sun rise in a blaze of colors over the horizon, casting its golden glow upon the shimmering waves. Kayak through mangrove forests teeming with exotic birds, or join local fishermen casting their nets in the traditional "bagan" technique. Enjoy fresh seafood feasts on the beach, savor tropical cocktails under the starlit sky, and let the rhythm of the ocean lull you into blissful serenity.

2.4 Beyond the Coast: Exploring Lombok's Enchanting Rice Terraces and Villages

Venturing beyond the shoreline, Lombok's interior unveils a tapestry of emerald rice terraces that cascade down verdant hillsides. These intricate landscapes, sculpted by generations of farmers, whisper stories of tradition and harmony with nature. Hike through lush valleys, where emerald rice paddies shimmer under the sun, and meet the friendly farmers who nurture the land. Learn about the intricate irrigation systems and ancient rituals tied to rice cultivation, gaining a deeper appreciation for the island's agricultural heart.

Nestled amidst the rice fields, Lombok's villages offer a glimpse into the island's authentic soul. Step back in time in traditional

Sasak villages, where thatched-roof houses huddle amongst coconut palms and villagers still practice time-honored customs. Witness women weaving vibrant "ikat" textiles, hear the rhythmic pounding of rice mortars, and experience the warm hospitality offered with genuine smiles. Attend a village ceremony, learn a few Bahasa Indonesia phrases, and indulge in local delicacies like "bebek plecing" spicy duck or "sate lilit" minced meat skewers.

Lombok's villages are not just museums of tradition; they are vibrant communities buzzing with life. Explore bustling markets overflowing with colorful fruits, handcrafted souvenirs, and the earthy aroma of spices. Witness children playing traditional games, attend a cockfight in an open field (be mindful of local customs), and join the festive spirit of village celebrations. Each interaction, each conversation, unveils a new facet of Lombok's culture, leaving you enriched and connected to the island's beating heart.

Chapter Three

Cultural Delights of Lombok

3.1 The Rhythm of Sasak Traditions: Experiencing Lombok's Vibrant Art, Music, and Dance

Lombok's heart beats to the vibrant rhythm of Sasak traditions, a tapestry woven from intricate art, mesmerizing music, and captivating dance. Stepping into this cultural realm is like entering a living museum, where ancestral customs come alive in every village and celebration.

Art Awaits in Every Corner: Wander through local markets and witness the intricate beauty of "ikat" textiles. These vibrant fabrics, woven with generations-old techniques, explode with a kaleidoscope of colors and patterns, each thread telling a story. Watch as nimble fingers work ancient looms, transforming threads into wearable art that adorns homes and bodies alike. Beyond textiles, discover intricate wood carvings depicting mythical creatures and everyday objects, or be mesmerized by the delicate dance of silver jewelry crafted by skilled artisans.

Music that Stirs the Soul: The air of Lombok vibrates with the haunting melodies of the "gendang beleq." This bamboo ensemble, with its rhythmic pounding and hypnotic chanting, transports you to another realm. Witness villagers come together during ceremonies, their bodies swaying in unison to the beat, invoking ancestral spirits and celebrating life's milestones. From the melancholic tones of the "rindik" bamboo flute to the percussive energy of the "bebele" bamboo xylophone, each instrument sings a unique song of Sasak culture.

Dance that Tells a Story: Stories unfold not just through words but through the rhythmic movements of traditional Sasak dance. Witness the fiery twirls of the "rudat," where warriors reenact ancient battles with fierce stomping and synchronized chants. Be captivated by the graceful swaying of the "ronggeng" as young women tell tales of love and longing through elegant gestures and expressive eyes. Every movement, every beat, speaks volumes about Sasak beliefs, history, and cultural identity.

Immerse yourself in these cultural expressions. Learn a few steps of the "rudat," attempt to weave a simple "ikat" pattern, or try your hand at playing the "rindik." These experiences, far beyond passive observation, forge a deeper connection with Lombok's vibrant spirit.

3.2 Unveiling the Secrets of Wastra: Immerse in Lombok's Textile Weaving Artisanship

The word "wastra" whispers of more than just fabric; it speaks of a profound art form, a cultural legacy woven into the very fabric of Lombok's identity. "Ikat" weaving lies at the heart of wastra, a complex and painstaking technique that transforms threads into vibrant masterpieces.

Stepping into the World of Ikat: Visit a traditional Sasak village and witness the magic unfold. Watch as women, their fingers moving with practiced ease, thread intricate patterns onto looms. Learn about the natural dyes extracted from plants and minerals, each color imbued with symbolic meaning. From the fiery reds of hibiscus to the calming blues of indigo, the palette of "ikat" reflects the island's vibrant soul.

Decoding the Language of Patterns: Every swirl, every geometric design, tells a story in the language of "ikat." Traditional motifs depicting flora, fauna, and even spiritual symbols convey cultural beliefs and aspirations. Learn to decipher these stories, appreciate the hidden message woven into every thread.

From Loom to Community: "Ikat" weaving isn't just an art form; it's the lifeblood of many Lombok communities. Visit weaving cooperatives and discover the vital role "ikat" plays in women's empowerment and financial independence. Witness their passion, their dedication to this age-old tradition, and their pride in preserving their cultural heritage.

Embrace the Experience: Beyond observation, immerse yourself in the world of "ikat." Try your hand at weaving a simple pattern, understand the significance of colors and motifs, and connect with the artisans who pour their souls into this art form. Take home a piece of "wastra" not just as a souvenir, but as a portal to Lombok's vibrant culture, a story woven in threads of tradition and artistry.

3.3 A Culinary Adventure: Savoring the Authentic Flavors of Lombok Cuisine

Embark on a sensory journey through Lombok's vibrant culinary landscape. The island's cuisine is a harmonious blend of Indonesian influences, boasting unique flavors and dishes that tantalize the taste buds and offer a glimpse into local traditions.

Spice Up Your Life: Step into a bustling warung (local eatery) and let the intoxicating aroma of fresh herbs and aromatic spices guide your senses. Lombok's cuisine celebrates chilies, ginger, turmeric, and lemongrass, creating warm, comforting curries like the fiery "plecing kangkong" (water spinach salad) or the aromatic "bebek plecing" (spicy duck). Don't be surprised by the occasional sting; embrace the bold flavors and discover the delicate balance of spice and sweetness that defines Lombok's culinary identity.

Beyond the Rendang: While rendang may be the queen of Indonesian cuisine, Lombok offers a diverse repertoire of dishes waiting to be savored. Sample the tangy "sate lilit" (minced meat skewers grilled on lemongrass stalks), the fragrant "ayam bakar taliwang" (grilled chicken marinated in turmeric and chilies), or the refreshing "bebalung terung" (eggplant soup). Venture beyond the tourist hotspots and discover village specialties like the smoky "bebek betutu" (black duck marinated in spices) or the hearty "opor bebele" (spicy jackfruit stew). Each dish whispers a story about local ingredients, traditional cooking methods, and the island's unique culinary heritage.

Sweet Endings: No meal is complete without indulging in Lombok's sweet finale. From the sticky-sweet "pisang goreng" (fried bananas) sprinkled with cinnamon to the creamy "dadar gulung" (coconut pancakes filled with palm sugar), every bite bursts with tropical flavors. Refresh your palate with a glass of freshly squeezed fruit juice or indulge in a scoop of homemade ice cream, savoring the island's bounty under the warm sun.

Dine Like a Local: Skip the fancy restaurants and embrace the authentic experience of warung dining. Share a table with friendly locals, delve into conversations through hand gestures and smiles, and learn about the cultural significance behind each dish. Don't be afraid to try something new, ask questions, and appreciate the warmth and hospitality that accompanies every meal.

3.4 Temple Tales: Discovering Lombok's Sacred Hindu and Islamic Heritage

Lombok's spiritual tapestry is woven from threads of both Hinduism and Islam, creating a unique landscape of diverse religious traditions. Witness this harmony in the island's sacred sites, where ancient temples whisper tales of the past and mosques stand as monuments to faith.

Hindu Echoes in Stone: Embark on a journey through time at the majestic Mayura temple, a testament to Balinese influence. Marvel at the intricate carvings and towering gates, echoing the stories of Hindu mythology. Climb the steep steps to the inner sanctum, feel the serene atmosphere, and witness the vibrant ceremonies that come alive during festivals like Nyepi (Balinese New Year).

Mosques: Pillars of Faith: Explore the serene beauty of Lombok's mosques, reflecting the island's strong Islamic traditions. Step into the Masjid Agung Selaparang, the oldest mosque in Lombok, and admire its elegant blend of Arabic and Javanese architectural styles.

Witness the vibrant prayer calls that echo through the air, join the faithful during Ramadan celebrations, and experience the deep spirituality that permeates these sacred spaces.

Harmony amidst Diversity: Beyond the architectural marvels, discover the spirit of tolerance and interfaith harmony that defines Lombok. Witness Hindus and Muslims participating in each other's festivals, sharing traditions, and living in peaceful coexistence.

This respect for diverse beliefs is an integral part of the island's identity, offering a valuable lesson in celebrating differences and finding common ground.

Embrace the Spiritual Journey: Delve deeper into Lombok's religious life by attending a ceremony, learning about local customs and beliefs, and engaging in respectful conversations with worshippers. These experiences offer a glimpse into the island's soul, fostering understanding and appreciation for the richness of its spiritual heritage.

Chapter Four

Adventures for Every Thrill Seeker

4.1 Surfing Paradise: Conquering Lombok's Epic Waves and Hidden Breaks

For adrenaline junkies and wave chasers, Lombok beckons with an irresistible siren song. The island's coastline boasts a treasure trove of world-class surf breaks, catering to every level, from seasoned veterans tearing into Gerupuk's monstrous barrels to excited beginners catching their first ride on Selong's gentle rollers.

Carve Your Lines on World-Class Breaks: Gerupuk Beach is Lombok's surfing crown jewel, a magnet for experienced riders seeking long, powerful righthanders that peel down the reef like liquid emeralds. Challenge yourself on Desert Point, renowned for its hollow tubes and demanding conditions, or test your skills on the reef breaks of Seger Beach, where consistent swells offer thrilling rides.

Unveil Hidden Gems: Beyond the well-known spots, Lombok hides a tapestry of secret breaks waiting to be discovered. Rent a local boat and venture past the crowds to untouched coves where untouched waves roll onto perfect, uncrowded sand. Ask local surfers for their insider tips, embrace the spirit of adventure, and carve your own line on Lombok's hidden gems.

Surfing Beyond the Board: The surfing experience in Lombok extends beyond chasing waves. Immerse yourself in the laid-back surf culture, where camaraderie reigns supreme. Share stories and tips with fellow surfers, learn from local surf guides, and participate in community events like beach cleanups and surf competitions. Embrace the island's relaxed pace, savor fresh seafood feasts after a session, and let the rhythm of the ocean lull you into a state of blissful post-surf zen.

4.2 Diving into Coral Kingdoms: Exploring Lombok's Underwater World of Rich Biodiversity

Beneath the turquoise waves of Lombok, a kaleidoscope of life unfolds. Coral reefs teeming with vibrant colors and exotic creatures beckon divers to a world of wonder and adventure. Whether you're a seasoned underwater explorer or a curious novice, Lombok's dive sites offer experiences that will stay etched in your memory.

Dive into Coral Cathedrals: Witness the vibrant tapestry of life swirling around the magnificent Gili Nanggu reef. Schools of rainbow-colored fish dart through coral canyons, majestic turtles glide by, and playful dolphins might even make an appearance. Explore underwater sculptures at the Sirens Reef, an artificial wonder attracting diverse marine life, or marvel at the awe-inspiring underwater pinnacles of Manta Point, where graceful manta rays gracefully glide through the currents.

Macro Magic: Lombok's reefs are more than just a spectacle; they're a haven for hidden treasures. Gear up for macro dives and discover a symphony of colors and textures hidden in the nooks and crannies of the coral. Spot tiny nudibranchs, shy pipefish camouflaged amongst the foliage, or witness the intricate dance of shrimp cleaning larger marine life. Every dive promises new surprises, reminding you of the intricate beauty hidden beneath the surface.

Beyond the Reefs: Lombok's underwater adventures extend beyond the reefs. Drift dives along walls laden with soft corals offer exhilarating encounters with pelagic creatures like tuna, sharks, and even whales sharks. Visit Shark Point, where nurse sharks slumber in the sand, or venture to Manta Point on full moon nights to witness a mesmerizing ballet of feeding manta rays. With careful observation and respect for marine life, these encounters offer unforgettable glimpses into the ocean's majestic predators.

Responsible Diving: Remember, you're a guest in this underwater kingdom. Practice responsible diving techniques, minimize your impact on the environment, and choose eco-friendly dive operators. Learn about coral conservation efforts and contribute to protecting this precious ecosystem. By being mindful and respectful, you'll ensure that future generations can experience the magic of Lombok's underwater world.

4.3 Trekking through Time: Embarking on Historical Trails and Cultural Journeys

Lombok's landscapes whisper stories of its past, inviting you to embark on treks that bridge the gap between past and present. Hike through verdant valleys where ancient Hindu temples lie hidden amidst the jungle, their intricately carved stones speaking of forgotten dynasties. Follow village paths used for centuries by farmers, immersing yourself in their rhythm of life and witnessing the timeless traditions that still thrive.

Walk amongst Legends: Trek through the mystical Rinjani caldera, where myths and legends intertwine with breathtaking scenery. Visit the Pura Semeru Agung, a sacred Hindu temple perched on the slopes, and soak in the mystical atmosphere. Ascend to the crater rim and gaze upon the turquoise Segara Anak lake, said to be the abode of spirits. Every step echoes with the footsteps of pilgrims and warriors who walked this path before you, connecting you to the island's rich historical tapestry.

Unearth Hidden Villages: Venture beyond the tourist trail and discover Lombok's hidden villages, untouched by the tide of mass tourism. Hike through valleys dotted with traditional Sasak houses, their thatched roofs blending seamlessly with the landscape. Engage with friendly locals, learn about their ancient customs and rituals, and witness the art of woodcarving or "ikat" weaving passed down through generations. Each encounter unveils a new facet of Lombok's cultural mosaic, leaving you enriched and connected to its vibrant soul.

History on Two Wheels: Embrace a slower pace and explore Lombok's historic sites on two wheels. Cycle through charming villages, pause at roadside shrines adorned with colorful offerings, and follow quiet paths leading to hidden temples. Visit the Mayura temple complex, its architectural splendor revealing the island's Balinese influences. As you cycle, the landscape unfolds at your own rhythm, inviting you to absorb the local sights and sounds and connect with the island's spirit on a deeper level.

4.4 Beyond the Ordinary: Caving, Cycling, and Kayaking through Lombok's Diverse Terrain

Lombok's adventures extend beyond the expected, offering experiences that push your boundaries and ignite your sense of wonder.

Delve into the Earth's Mysteries: Embark on a spelunking adventure and explore the hidden depths of Lombok's caves. Navigate through chambers adorned with stalactites and stalagmites, their shapes hinting at fantastical creatures and forgotten myths. Discover ancient inscriptions hinting at past civilizations, or witness the unique cave fauna that thrives in this perpetual darkness. This subterranean journey through time promises an unforgettable thrill.

Pedal through Paradise: Lace up your shoes and conquer Lombok's challenging yet rewarding cycling routes. Climb through lush hillsides, navigate scenic coastal paths, and traverse verdant rice paddies. Cycle alongside locals, sharing smiles and conversations, and soak in the breathtaking vistas that unfold around every bend. From leisurely village explorations to adrenaline-pumping downhill rides, Lombok's diverse terrain caters to every cycling enthusiast.

Paddle into Serenity: Glide through the calm waters of Lombok's mangroves and hidden bays on a kayaking adventure. Witness the intricate ecosystem teeming with life, from playful monkeys swinging from the trees to colorful fish darting through the shallows. Navigate hidden canals, listen to the symphony of the forest, and discover secret coves accessible only by water. This peaceful journey offers a unique perspective on Lombok's natural beauty and a chance to reconnect with nature's tranquility.

Chapter Five

Unveiling Lombok's Gilis: Island Hopping Paradise

Lombok's crown jewels lie scattered like emeralds upon the turquoise waves - the Gili Islands. These three tiny havens offer distinct personalities, beckoning travelers with their unique blend of charm, adventure, and laid-back island vibes.

5.1 Gili Trawangan: A Buzzing Hive of Activity and Party Vibes

Gili Trawangan, the largest and liveliest of the Gili trio, pulsates with an infectious energy. Backpackers flock to its shores, drawn by the vibrant nightlife, budget-friendly accommodation, and endless activities. Dive into the bustling atmosphere of its main strip, lined with bars, restaurants, and shops selling everything from souvenirs to surfboards.

Party Under the Stars: As the sun dips below the horizon, Gili Trawangan transforms into a party paradise. Beachfront bars come alive with music, fire dancers twirl amidst crackling flames, and laughter spills onto the sandy dance floor. Let loose to the rhythm of international DJs, sip on tropical cocktails under the starlit sky, and dance the night away amidst a vibrant crowd.

Beyond the Buzz: Don't let the party scene fool you; Gili Trawangan offers more than just late-night revelry. Hike or bike around the island's perimeter, discovering hidden coves and serene beaches away from the crowds. Learn to surf on gentle waves, explore the vibrant coral reefs on a snorkeling or diving trip, or indulge in a pampering spa treatment. Gili Trawangan caters to every mood, from adrenaline-pumping activities to quiet moments of solitude.

5.2 Gili Air: Tranquil Escape for Relaxation and Romance

In stark contrast to its boisterous neighbor, Gili Air whispers promises of serenity and romance. Escape the crowds and unwind on pristine beaches bathed in the golden glow of the setting sun. Stroll along the island's sandy paths, lined with boutique resorts and charming cafes, breathing in the scent of frangipani and fresh seafood.

Embrace the Tranquility: Gili Air's relaxed pace invites you to slow down and reconnect with yourself. Take a yoga class on the beach, indulge in a rejuvenating massage, or simply lie back on a hammock and soak in the tranquil atmosphere. Spend your days snorkeling amongst colorful fish in crystal-clear waters or kayaking through mangrove forests teeming with life. This island paradise offers a haven for those seeking peace and quietude.

Romantic Rendezvous: Gili Air sets the perfect stage for a romantic getaway. Enjoy candlelit dinners on the beach, stargaze hand-in-hand on the sand, or rent a private boat for a sunset cruise across the glistening sea. Celebrate your love with a traditional Sasak ceremony, witness the magical bioluminescent plankton illuminating the night, or simply savor the intimacy of being surrounded by paradise.

Island Hopping Delights: No Gili experience is complete without island hopping. Embark on a day trip to Gili Meno, the smallest of the islands, and discover its secluded coves and idyllic atmosphere. Explore the underwater world at Shark Point near Gili Trawangan, or witness the majestic turtles nesting on Gili Meno's shores. Each island offers its own unique charm, creating an unforgettable island-hopping adventure.

5.3 Gili Meno: Honeymoon Haven and Snorkeling Sanctuary

Gili Meno, the smallest and most laid-back of the Gili trio, is a haven for honeymooners, snorkelers, and those seeking ultimate tranquility. Its pristine beaches stretch like silken ribbons, kissed by the turquoise embrace of the sea. Lush greenery whispers secrets in the gentle breeze, and the air vibrates with the rhythm of serenity.

Honeymoon Bliss: Gili Meno is where romance takes center stage. Luxurious beachfront villas offer secluded havens for couples, promising candlelit dinners on the sand, private plunge pools overlooking the ocean, and personalized spa treatments. Celebrate your love with a traditional Sasak wedding ceremony, witness the breathtaking sunset from a private boat, or simply lose yourselves in the island's enchanting embrace.

Snorkeling Symphony: Beneath the crystal-clear waters of Gili Meno lies a vibrant underwater world teeming with life. Grab your snorkel and mask and dive into a kaleidoscope of colors, corals, and exotic creatures. Glide alongside graceful turtles, marvel at the shimmering dance of fish, and discover hidden coral gardens teeming with biodiversity. This snorkeling paradise promises unforgettable encounters with the wonders of the sea.

Beyond the Reef: Gili Meno offers more than just beach bliss and underwater adventures. Rent a bicycle and explore the island's interior, discovering hidden temples, serene lagoons, and verdant forests. Immerse yourself in the island's laid-back pace, learn to surf gentle waves, or simply relax in a hammock strung between palm trees, listening to the soothing rhythm of the waves. This island sanctuary invites you to disconnect, unwind, and reconnect with nature's gentle embrace.

5.4 Island Hopping Delights: Discovering the Untouched Charms of Smaller Gili Islands

Beyond the main trio, Lombok's Gili archipelago holds hidden gems waiting to be discovered. Venture beyond the tourist trail and embark on an island-hopping adventure that unveils untouched beaches, crystal-clear waters, and a sense of pristine solitude.

Gili Nanggu: This tiny island, accessible only by private boat, is a haven for luxury and seclusion. Eco-friendly resorts blend seamlessly with the landscape, offering overwater bungalows and private beaches where you can bask in the sun and revel in undisturbed peace. Dive into the vibrant coral reefs teeming with marine life, or explore the island's interior on a guided birdwatching tour.

Gili Kedis: This hidden gem is a sanctuary for nature lovers. Pristine beaches, untouched by development, stretch for miles, while turquoise waters beckon you to swim, snorkel, and explore the vibrant marine life. Immerse yourself in the island's rustic charm, stay in traditional bungalows, and experience the authentic spirit of Lombok's island life.

Gili Layar: This emerging island is a haven for surfers and divers. Untamed waves challenge experienced riders, while pristine reefs offer breathtaking encounters with marine life. Explore the island's growing infrastructure, dotted with charming cafes and boutique resorts, and discover a laid-back island vibe that blends adventure with relaxation.

Island Hopping Adventures: No Gili experience is complete without exploring the archipelago's diversity. Rent a private boat and hop from island to island, discovering hidden coves, snorkeling through untouched coral reefs, and enjoying picnics on pristine beaches. Each island offers a unique charm, creating an unforgettable island-hopping adventure that will leave you with memories to cherish.

Chapter Six

Lombok for Nature Lovers

Lombok's untamed beauty transcends beaches and turquoise waters. For nature enthusiasts, the island whispers promises of emerald forests, soaring birds, and breathtaking biodiversity. This chapter invites you to delve into Lombok's natural wonders, where adventure awaits around every bend.

6.1 Birdwatching Bonanza: Spotting Endemic Species in Lombok's National Parks

For avid birdwatchers, Lombok is a symphony of feathered friends. The island boasts diverse habitats, from lush rainforests to coastal wetlands, attracting a vibrant array of feathered residents and migratory visitors. Embark on a birdwatching adventure and discover a kaleidoscope of color and song.

Mount Rinjani National Park: Hike through the mist-shrouded slopes of Mount Rinjani, a haven for endemic species like the Rinjani scops owl and the Lombok spiderhunter. Listen for the melodic calls of the crested honey-eaters or witness the magnificent flight of the brahminy kite soaring above the verdant valleys.

Rinjani Wildlife Reserve: Venture into the lush rainforests of the Rinjani Wildlife Reserve, home to the critically endangered white-rumped shama and the elusive crested serpent-eagle. Trek through the jungle canopy, listening for the cacophony of bird calls and marveling at the vibrant plumage of exotic species.

South Lombok Mangroves: Paddle through the maze of mangrove forests in South Lombok, a sanctuary for waterbirds. Spot brightly colored kingfishers perched on branches, witness the graceful dance of herons wading in the shallows, and listen to the haunting calls of migratory shorebirds.

Beyond the Parks: Birdwatching adventures extend beyond designated areas. Keep your eyes peeled in rice paddies, where paddyfield pipits flit amongst the green shoots, or search for colorful sunbirds sipping nectar from blooming hibiscus flowers. Every corner of

Lombok offers a glimpse into the island's rich avian diversity.

6.2 Jungle Encounters: Trekking through Lush Rainforests and Spotting Exotic Wildlife

Lombok's rainforests are teeming with life, waiting to be discovered on foot. Lace up your boots and embark on a trekking adventure that will immerse you in the emerald embrace of the island's wild heart.

Senaru Crater Rim Trek: Conquer the challenging yet rewarding Senaru Crater Rim Trek, ascending Mount Rinjani's slopes past diverse forests and breathtaking vistas. Encounter curious monkeys swinging through the trees, listen for the calls of unseen gibbons, and spot colorful butterflies flitting through the dappled sunlight.

Sesaot Forest: Explore the mystical Sesaot Forest, a wonderland of towering trees and hidden waterfalls. Navigate through mossy trails, spot shy deer amidst the foliage, and witness the impressive hornbill birds flitting across the canopy.

Jernuk Waterfall: Trek through the verdant valley leading to Jernuk Waterfall, a hidden gem cascading into a turquoise pool. Cool off in the refreshing waters, listen to the symphony of the jungle, and enjoy the serenity of this untouched paradise.

Jungle Ethics: Remember, you're a guest in this delicate ecosystem. Tread lightly, avoid littering, and respect the wildlife. Choose responsible tours that prioritize conservation and support local communities. By adopting sustainable practices, you ensure that future generations can experience the magic of Lombok's rainforests.

6.3 Marine Marvels: Conservation Efforts and Protecting Lombok's Underwater Treasures

Beyond the breathtaking beauty of Lombok's coral reefs lies a story of resilience and hope. Overfishing, pollution, and unsustainable tourism practices have taken their toll on this precious ecosystem. However, a wave of conservation efforts is rising, promising a brighter future for Lombok's marine marvels.

Coral Guardians: Dive into the heart of conservation initiatives led by passionate individuals and organizations. Learn about coral restoration projects that nurture damaged reefs back to life, witness the dedication of dive operators committed to sustainable practices, and volunteer your time in beach cleanups or educational programs.

Community Empowered: Sustainable tourism goes beyond individual actions. By choosing eco-friendly resorts and tour operators who support local communities and conservation efforts, you empower positive change. Immerse yourself in cultural experiences led by local guides, source souvenirs from handcrafted workshops, and choose locally-sourced meals that support Lombok's farmers and fishermen.

Responsible Diving: Be a mindful underwater explorer. Practice buoyancy control to avoid damaging coral formations, choose reef-safe sunscreen to protect marine life, and avoid touching marine creatures. Support dive operators who educate their guests about sustainable diving practices and actively participate in conservation initiatives.

Beyond the Reefs: Protect the fragile balance of Lombok's ecosystem by leaving no trace on land. Reduce your plastic footprint, choose eco-friendly toiletries, and respect local customs and traditions. Every small step contributes to a more sustainable future for this island paradise.

6.4 Sustainable Travel: Responsible Tourism Practices for a Greener Lombok

Lombok's beauty beckons us, but responsible tourism ensures that future generations can experience its magic. By actively embracing sustainability practices, we minimize our impact and contribute to a greener future for the island.

Minimizing Footprint: Travel light and choose accommodations that prioritize energy efficiency and waste reduction. Opt for local transportation options like bicycles or public buses and minimize your reliance on air-conditioned vehicles. Pack reusable water bottles and bags to eliminate single-use plastics, and choose eco-friendly sunscreens and toiletries.

Cultural Sensitivity: Embrace Lombok's rich cultural tapestry with respect. Dress modestly when visiting religious sites, learn basic Bahasa Indonesia phrases, and be mindful of local customs and traditions. Support local artisans by purchasing handcrafted souvenirs and participate in cultural experiences without being intrusive or exploitative.

Supporting the Community: Choose locally-run tours and homestays, directly benefiting the Lombok people. Learn about local initiatives and donate to organizations working towards environmental protection and community development. Every ethical interaction creates a ripple effect, leading to a more prosperous and sustainable future for the island.

Become a Lombok Ambassador: Share your responsible travel experiences with others, inspiring them to adopt sustainable practices. Advocate for eco-friendly tourism choices, support conservation efforts, and spread awareness about the importance of protecting Lombok's natural beauty and cultural heritage.

Chapter Seven

Family Fun in Lombok

Lombok isn't just a haven for thrill-seekers and honeymooners; it's also a paradise for families seeking adventure, laughter, and memories that will last a lifetime. From splashing fun on pristine beaches to cultural immersions that spark curiosity, this chapter invites you to discover the island's endless possibilities for family-friendly adventures.

7.1 Splashing Adventures: Water Parks, Beaches, and Family-Friendly Activities

Sunshine, turquoise waters, and endless laughter - Lombok's coastline beckons families to create unforgettable memories.

Water Park Paradise: Let loose at the Energii Water Park, Lombok's premier water playground. Race down thrilling slides, splash in wave pools, and conquer the challenging climbing wall. Younger children can frolic in dedicated play areas, while families unite at the lazy river, soaking up the tropical sunshine together.

Beach Bonanza: No Lombok family adventure is complete without building sandcastles and splashing in the waves. Discover Tanjung Aan Beach, a picture-perfect stretch of golden sand with gentle waves ideal for young swimmers. For snorkeling adventures, venture to Selong Belanak Beach, where colorful fish dart amongst calm reefs. Take a boat trip to the Gili Islands and let your kids marvel at the underwater wonders through glass-bottom boats.

Beyond the Beach: Lombok offers more than just aquatic fun. Hike to the Benang Stokal and Benang Kelambu waterfalls, where hidden pools beckon for refreshing dips. Rent bicycles and explore the charming villages around Mount Rinjani, stopping for picnic lunches amidst breathtaking scenery. Take a horseback riding adventure through rice paddies or let your kids learn to surf gentle waves on Selong Beach.

7.2 Educational Escapades: Cultural Learning Experiences and Museums for Kids

Spark your children's curiosity and broaden their horizons with immersive cultural experiences in Lombok.

Museum Adventures: Visit the Narmada Botanic Garden and Museum, where vibrant flora intertwines with ancient artifacts, telling stories of Lombok's history and traditions. At the Pura Agung Narmada temple complex, kids can marvel at the intricately carved stone structures and learn about Hindu beliefs. In Mataram, the Sasak Village Museum showcases traditional crafts and daily life, offering a glimpse into the island's rich cultural heritage.

Cooking Classes: Bond over a fun activity and learn about local cuisine by joining a family cooking class. Master the art of preparing delicious "bebek bakar" (grilled duck), whip up fragrant "plecing kangkung" (water spinach salad), and create playful desserts like "dadar gulung" (coconut crepes). These hands-on experiences turn mealtimes into cultural adventures.

Wayang Puppets: Introduce your children to the magic of "wayang kulit," traditional shadow puppet plays. Immerse yourselves in the captivating stories, intricate puppet designs, and the mesmerizing gamelan music that accompanies each performance. This unique cultural experience will spark imaginations and leave a lasting impression.

Cultural Workshops: Let your kids unleash their creativity by participating in traditional craft workshops. Learn how to weave "ikat" textiles, carve wood like skilled Sasak artisans, or paint intricate batik patterns. These interactive sessions offer valuable lessons in cultural appreciation and leave your family with cherished souvenirs.

7.3 Wildlife Encounters: Zoos, Animal Sanctuaries, and Responsible Wildlife Interactions

Beyond beaches and cultural immersions, Lombok offers incredible opportunities for families to connect with the island's diverse wildlife. However, responsible interactions are crucial to ensure animal welfare and preserve Lombok's natural beauty.

Zoo Adventures: Embark on a fascinating journey at the Narmada Zoo, where families can observe Sumatran tigers, playful orangutans, and majestic Komodo dragons in spacious enclosures. Choose zoos that prioritize animal welfare, offering enriching environments and ethical conservation practices.

Animal Sanctuaries: For a more intimate experience, visit wildlife sanctuaries dedicated to rescuing and rehabilitating animals. Learn about the stories of rescued monkeys, majestic birds, and playful otters at the Lombok Wildlife Park. Contribute to conservation efforts through responsible interactions that focus on education and respect.

Responsible Wildlife Interactions: Remember, animals are not props for entertainment. Avoid activities that exploit or harm wildlife, such as riding elephants or interacting with endangered species in unnatural settings. Choose ethical encounters that prioritize animal welfare and promote conservation awareness.

7.4 Family-Friendly Accommodation: Choosing the Perfect Resort for Fun and Relaxation

Finding the perfect Lombok accommodation for your family is key to a stress-free and enjoyable vacation.

Beachfront Bliss: Embrace the island vibes by opting for a beachfront resort nestled along pristine shores. Let your kids build sandcastles, splash in the waves, and participate in organized beach activities while you unwind under swaying palm trees. Look for resorts offering dedicated kids' clubs, supervised playgrounds, and family-friendly pools to keep everyone entertained.

Cultural Immersion: Experience the charm of Lombok's villages by choosing a traditional homestay. Learn about Sasak customs and traditions from your hosts, enjoy homemade meals prepared with fresh local ingredients, and let your children play with village kids, creating lasting friendships. Homestays offer an authentic cultural experience with a touch of local hospitality.

Eco-Friendly Retreats: Choose resorts committed to sustainability and environmental responsibility. Opt for eco-certified accommodations that utilize renewable energy, minimize waste, and support local communities. Teach your kids about eco-friendly practices while enjoying comfortable amenities and breathtaking natural surroundings.

All-Inclusive Adventures: Simplify your vacation with an all-inclusive resort package. Enjoy buffet meals, unlimited drinks, and access to a variety of activities, from watersports and kids' clubs to cultural shows and theme nights. This carefree option allows families to relax and focus on having fun together.

Remember: Consider your family's needs and preferences when choosing accommodation. Look for age-appropriate activities, kid-friendly menus, and safe swimming areas. Don't hesitate to contact the resort beforehand to inquire about specific amenities and services that cater to families.

Chapter Eight

Lombok Beyond the Tourist Trail

Lombok whispers its secrets to those who dare to venture beyond the well-trodden path. This chapter invites you to delve into the island's hidden gems, where untouched beaches beckon with pristine sands and authentic experiences offer a glimpse into the soul of Lombok.

8.1 Secret Beaches and Hidden Gems: Discovering Off-the-Beaten-Path Paradises

Escape the crowds and discover your own private paradise on Lombok's secret shores.

Tanjung Aan's Secret Coves: Venture beyond the main stretch of Tanjung Aan Beach and stumble upon secluded coves nestled amidst towering cliffs. Swim in turquoise pools carved into the rocks, sunbathe on pristine sands untouched by footprints, and let the rhythm of the waves lull you into serenity.

Seger Beach's Hidden Beauty: Tucked away beyond a winding path, Seger Beach unfolds like a secret paradise. Its golden sands stretch for miles, kissed by gentle waves ideal for swimming and splashing. Rent a surfboard and conquer the rolling swells, or simply relax under the shade of palm trees and soak in the tranquility.

Pinky Beach's Coral Symphony: Sail to the remote shores of Pinky Beach, named for its coral fragments that tinge the sand a blush rose. Snorkel or dive into a kaleidoscope of marine life hiding amidst the coral reefs, or witness the breathtaking sunset painting the sky in fiery hues.

Beyond the Coast: Lombok's hidden treasures extend beyond the coastline. Hike through the verdant foothills of Mount Rinjani to uncover hidden waterfalls cascading into turquoise pools. Explore the lush Senaru jungle, where ancient temples lie hidden amidst the foliage, and discover the serenity of untouched nature.

Remember: Respect the local communities and environment when venturing off the beaten path. Avoid littering, dress modestly when visiting religious sites, and ask permission before entering private property.

8.2 Local Markets and Authentic Experiences: Immerse in the Daily Life of Lombok's Villages

Experience the spirit of Lombok by stepping into the vibrant pulse of its local markets.

Mataram's Pasar Tradisional: Dive into the bustling heart of Mataram's traditional market. Haggle for colorful sarongs, handcrafted souvenirs, and fresh tropical fruits. Immerse yourself in the cacophony of bartering voices and savor the aroma of local delicacies wafting from street food stalls.

Tetebatu Vegetable Market: Witness the colorful tapestry of Lombok's agricultural bounty at the Tetebatu Vegetable Market. Rows upon rows of vibrant produce spill forth, from glistening mangoes and juicy pineapples to fragrant herbs and exotic spices. Engage with friendly farmers, learn about local agricultural practices, and pick up fresh ingredients for a delicious home-cooked meal.

Sasak Village Encounters: Visit a traditional Sasak village and discover the island's rich cultural heritage. Learn about their unique architecture, watch artisans weaving "ikat" textiles, and witness the mesmerizing "gendang beleq" bamboo dance performance. Savor a home-cooked meal prepared with local ingredients and connect with the warm hospitality of the Sasak people.

Cooking Classes and Workshops: Master the art of preparing authentic Lombok dishes by participating in a cooking class. Learn to grill "bebek bakar" (duck), whip up a tangy "plecing kangkung" salad, and create melt-in-your-mouth "dadar gulung" (coconut crepes). These interactive experiences offer a delicious taste of local culture.

Remember: Approach these authentic experiences with respect and curiosity. Be mindful of local customs and traditions, dress modestly, and refrain from taking intrusive photographs. Let yourself be a guest in their world and embrace the genuine warmth of Lombok's people.

8.3 Homestays and Cultural Exchanges: Staying with Locals and Experiencing True Lombok Hospitality

For an immersive experience beyond resort walls, consider swapping conventional accommodation for a homestay in a traditional Sasak village. This chapter invites you to step into the heart of Lombok's culture, living alongside locals, sharing meals, and discovering the warmth of true Lombok hospitality.

Traditional Charm: Immerse yourself in the beauty of Sasak architecture, staying in houses built with natural materials and adorned with intricate decorations. Awaken to the crowing of roosters and the gentle breeze rustling through palm trees, a stark contrast to the bustle of tourist hotspots.

Everyday Rhythms: Experience the pace of village life, joining your hosts in their daily activities. Help tend the vegetable garden, learn to weave "ikat" textiles, or cook traditional dishes alongside grandmothers sharing ancestral recipes. Witness the intricate community rituals and celebrations, becoming part of their vibrant tapestry.

Cultural Feast: Savor authentic Lombok cuisine prepared with fresh local ingredients. Learn the secrets of "bebek bakar" (grilled duck), indulge in spicy "plecing kangkung" (water spinach salad), and delight in sweet "dadar gulung" (coconut crepes). Sharing meals with your hosts fosters meaningful connections and allows you to truly appreciate the flavors of Lombok.

Language Bridges: Don't let language barriers limit your experience. Use gestures, smiles, and basic Bahasa Indonesia phrases to create a bond with your hosts. Learn a few words each day, immersing yourself in the local language and building bridges of understanding.

Remember: Respect local customs and traditions. Dress modestly, be mindful of religious practices, and ask permission before entering private spaces. Offer your help with daily chores, showing appreciation for their hospitality.

8.4 Volunteering Opportunities: Contributing to Conservation Efforts and Local Communities

Give back to Lombok and create a lasting impact by participating in volunteering opportunities. These experiences allow you to connect with the island's challenges and contribute to its future.

Marine Conservation: Join projects restoring damaged coral reefs, cleaning beaches, and educating locals about sustainable fishing practices. Learn from marine biologists and contribute to preserving Lombok's underwater treasures for future generations.

Community Development: Support initiatives empowering local communities, such as building schools, teaching English to children, or assisting with agricultural projects. Share your skills and knowledge, fostering meaningful connections and leaving a lasting positive impact.

Wildlife Rescue: Lend a hand at animal sanctuaries caring for rescued monkeys, birds, and other wildlife. Learn about rehabilitation efforts and contribute to ensuring the wellbeing of Lombok's diverse fauna.

Cultural Preservation: Assist in workshops that preserve traditional Sasak crafts, dances, and music. Help document folklore and stories, ensuring these cultural treasures are passed down to future generations.

Remember: Choose programs aligned with your interests and skills. Research reputable organizations and ensure your contribution is ethical and sustainable. Respect local cultures and traditions, offering your skills with humility and genuine desire to help.

Chapter Nine

Essential Information for Your Lombok Trip

Planning your perfect Lombok adventure requires navigating essential logistics. This chapter equips you with the knowledge to ensure a smooth and hassle-free experience, from visas and currency to getting around and staying connected.

9.1 Visa Requirements and Immigration Procedures

Before packing your bags, research entry requirements based on your citizenship. Many nationalities enjoy visa-free entry for 30 days upon arrival at Lombok International Airport or select seaports. However, ensure your passport has at least six months' validity and two blank pages for entry stamps.

For stays exceeding 30 days, apply for a tourist visa at your nearest Indonesian Embassy or Consulate before traveling. Provide necessary documents like passport photos, a completed visa application form, and proof of travel and accommodation bookings. Processing times can vary, so plan accordingly.

Remember, visa regulations are subject to change. Always check the latest information with official Indonesian government sources or a reputable travel agency before your trip.

9.2 Currency Exchange and Money Matters

Indonesia's official currency is the Indonesian rupiah (IDR). Exchange major currencies like USD, EUR, and GBP at authorized money changers or airport counters. Avoid street vendors due to potential scams and unfavorable rates. Withdraw cash from ATMs, but be aware of transaction fees and daily withdrawal limits.

To avoid carrying large amounts of cash, consider international credit cards accepted at most tourist restaurants and larger shops. However, smaller local vendors and rural areas may still require cash. Familiarize yourself with your bank's foreign transaction fees and inform them of your travel dates to avoid suspicious activity alerts.

For everyday purchases, bargaining is often expected at traditional markets and smaller shops. Start with a friendly offer and negotiate politely, respecting the vendor's livelihood. Tipping is not customary in Lombok, but a small gratuity for exceptional service is always appreciated.

Remember, plan your cash needs based on your activities and budget. Research average costs for accommodation, meals, transportation, and entrance fees to avoid last-minute surprises.

Additional Essential Information:

Flight Connections: Direct flights to Lombok International Airport are available from major Asian cities. Alternatively, consider connecting flights through Bali's Ngurah Rai International Airport.

Domestic Transportation: Taxis, metered and unmetered, are readily available at airports and tourist areas. For budget-friendly options, consider public buses or bemo (minibuses). Renting a motorbike offers independent exploration but requires local driving license and helmet use.

Staying Connected: Purchase a local SIM card for affordable mobile data and calls. Wi-Fi is available in most hotels and cafes, but connectivity might be limited in remote areas.

Travel Insurance: Invest in travel insurance that covers medical emergencies, flight cancellations, and lost luggage. Ensure your policy covers activities you plan to participate in, such as trekking or diving.

Respectful Travel: Dress modestly when visiting religious sites, be mindful of local customs, and learn basic Bahasa Indonesia phrases to engage with the locals.

By being well-informed and prepared, you can focus on creating unforgettable memories during your Lombok adventure.

9.3 Transportation Options and Getting Around Lombok

Exploring Lombok's diverse landscapes necessitates navigating its transportation options. This section unveils the efficient ways to hop between beaches, reach remote villages, and conquer rugged terrains, ensuring you experience every corner of the island.

Air Travel: Lombok International Airport is the main gateway, with direct flights from major Asian cities. Consider domestic connections via Bali's Ngurah Rai International Airport for further accessibility.

Land Transportation:

Taxis: Metered and unmetered taxis are readily available at airports and tourist hubs. Negotiate fares for unmetered taxis politely.

Bemos: These colorful minibusses offer budget-friendly travel on fixed routes, connecting villages and towns. Be prepared for crowded conditions.

Motorbike Rentals: Scooting around on a motorbike provides freedom and flexibility, but requires a local driving license and helmet use. Be cautious of traffic and road conditions.

Car Rentals: Renting a car offers comfort and convenience, especially for families or larger groups. Choose reputable rental companies and familiarize yourself with local traffic regulations.

Exploring the Gili Islands:

Public Boats: Regular public boats connect Lombok's mainland to the Gili Islands, offering an affordable and scenic journey.

Private Speedboats: Opt for private speed boats for quicker transfers, ideal for larger groups or time-constrained travelers.

Traditional "Jukung" Boats: Experience the charm of island hopping in a traditional "jukung" boat, the Gili Islanders' preferred mode of transport.

Remember: Plan your transportation in advance, especially for inter-island transfers during peak season. Factor in travel time and consider using a combination of options for a well-rounded experience.

9.4 Health and Safety Tips for a Safe and Healthy Journey

Prioritizing health and safety ensures a worry-free Lombok adventure. This section equips you with essential tips to protect your well-being and embrace responsible travel practices.

Vaccinations: Consult your doctor or a travel clinic about recommended vaccinations, including rabies, hepatitis A and B, and typhoid fever. Consider additional vaccines based on your planned activities and itinerary.

Travel Insurance: Invest in comprehensive travel insurance covering medical emergencies, flight cancellations, and lost luggage. Choose a policy that aligns with your activities, such as diving or trekking.

Sun Protection: Lombok's tropical sun can be intense. Use sunscreen with SPF 30 or higher, wear protective clothing and hats, and seek shade during peak sun hours.

Drinking Water: Stick to bottled water or purified water sources to avoid stomach upsets. Avoid consuming ice unless you're confident of its origin.

Food Safety: Opt for freshly cooked meals and restaurants with good hygiene practices. Avoid street food vendors unless confident of their cleanliness.

Insect Repellent: Protect yourself from mosquito bites, especially during rainy season, by using insect repellent containing DEET.

Emergency Contact Numbers: Save the emergency contact numbers for police (110), ambulance (118), and fire department (119) on your phone.

Responsible Tourism: Respect local customs and traditions, dress modestly when visiting religious sites, and dispose of waste responsibly. Support local businesses and communities for a sustainable travel experience.

Remember: Be aware of your surroundings, avoid secluded areas at night, and trust your instincts. Stay informed about local weather conditions and potential hazards, especially during the rainy season.

By prioritizing health and safety, adopting responsible travel practices, and remaining vigilant, you can ensure a healthy and fulfilling Lombok adventure.

Chapter Ten

Memories that Last a Lifetime

As your Lombok adventure draws to a close, the essence of the island lingers, imprinted in your heart and mind. This chapter celebrates the memories you carry and suggests ways to preserve them, from capturing breathtaking scenes to sharing your story with the world.

10.1 Capturing the Essence of Lombok: Photography Tips and Souvenirs to Bring Home

Your photos become windows to your Lombok experience, transporting you back to sun-drenched beaches, volcanic peaks, and smiling faces. Here are some tips to capture the island's magic:

Embrace the Light: Lombok's golden sunrises and fiery sunsets paint spectacular

landscapes. Plan your photography outings around these times for dramatic lighting.
Go Beyond the Obvious: While iconic landmarks deserve a frame, capture the essence of Lombok in everyday moments – children playing on the beach, fishermen mending their nets, the steam rising from a steaming cup of "kopikoe."

Tell a Story: Use photos to weave a narrative of your journey. Include candid portraits of locals, close-ups of intricate details, and action shots that capture the island's vibrant energy.
Respect Your Surroundings: Be mindful of cultural sensitivities and avoid taking intrusive photographs. Ask permission before photographing people, especially in religious settings.

Beyond photographs, tangible souvenirs hold the scent of Lombok. Choose handcrafted treasures that tell a story, from intricate Sasak textiles and woven baskets to locally-made jewelry and batik paintings. Visit markets and workshops to connect with artisans and support their livelihood.

Remember, the most precious souvenirs are not physical objects, but the experiences you carry within. The laughter shared with new friends, the thrill of climbing Mount Rinjani, the solace found in a hidden beach cove – these moments become woven into the tapestry of your being, long after you leave Lombok.

10.2 Sharing Your Lombok Story: Travel Blogging and Social Media Inspiration

Let your voice echo the beauty of Lombok! Today's digital world offers platforms to share your experiences and inspire others.

Travel Blogging: Start a blog to chronicle your Lombok journey, detailing your adventures, practical tips, and cultural insights. Share captivating photos and stories, creating a virtual guide for future travelers.

Social Media Inspiration: Capture Instagram-worthy moments and share them on your favorite platforms. Use relevant hashtags, tag collaborators like hotels or tour operators, and interact with the travel community. Your story might spark someone else's Lombok adventure!

Responsible Storytelling: Be mindful of how you portray the island. Highlight its beauty and culture while advocating for responsible tourism practices. Choose ethical businesses, embrace sustainable choices, and promote respect for local communities.

Through storytelling, you become a bridge connecting Lombok to the world. Your experiences, captured in photos and words, inspire others to explore, connect, and contribute to the island's well-being.

Remember: Authenticity is key. Share your genuine perspectives, both the joys and challenges, to create a relatable and valuable narrative. Encourage responsible travel, cultural sensitivity, and respect for the environment.

As you bid farewell to Lombok, know that a part of you will forever remain within its palm-fringed shores and vibrant coral reefs. Carry the memories close, share your story with passion, and keep a piece of Lombok magic alive wherever you go.

10.3 Responsible Tourism: Minimizing Your Footprint and Leaving a Positive Impact

As your Lombok adventure unfolds, its breathtaking landscapes and vibrant culture captivate your senses. However, along with experiencing its beauty, comes the responsibility of minimizing your impact and leaving a positive footprint on the island.

Embracing Sustainability:

Reduce Plastic: Carry a reusable water bottle, bag, and food containers to eliminate single-use plastic. Choose eco-friendly toiletries and support businesses committed to sustainability.

Respect Wildlife: Avoid activities that exploit or harm animals. Choose ethical snorkeling and diving operators, and never touch or feed marine life. Support wildlife conservation efforts through responsible volunteering or donations.

Support Local Communities: Opt for locally-run accommodations and tours, directly benefiting the Lombok people. Learn basic Bahasa Indonesia phrases to engage with locals and purchase handcrafted souvenirs from artisans.

Minimize Waste: Recycle and dispose of waste responsibly. Avoid littering and educate others about the importance of protecting Lombok's natural beauty.

Respect Cultural Sensitivities: Dress modestly when visiting religious sites, be mindful of local customs and traditions, and ask permission before entering private spaces. Immerse yourself in the culture with respect and appreciation.

By making conscious choices, you can minimize your environmental footprint and contribute to Lombok's sustainable development. Remember, responsible tourism is not just a trend; it's a commitment to ensuring the island's magic thrives for future generations.

10.4 Until We Meet Again: Saying Goodbye to Lombok and Planning Your Next Return

As you bid farewell to Lombok, a bittersweet tug pulls at your heart. The sun-kissed beaches, the gentle rhythm of life, the warmth of the people – these memories become intertwined with a yearning to return.

Embracing the Farewell:

Express Gratitude: Thank your local hosts, guides, and anyone who enriched your experience. Leave a genuine review for businesses that exceeded your expectations.

Share Your Story: Capture your journey through photos, videos, and journal entries. These become keepsakes to revisit and tools to inspire others to discover Lombok's magic.

Stay Connected: Follow Lombok-based businesses and organizations on social media. Stay updated on the island's developments and opportunities to contribute, even from afar.

Planning Your Next Return:

Keep an Open Heart: Stay open to new experiences and adventures on your next Lombok journey. Explore different regions, dive deeper into cultural encounters, and discover hidden gems you might have missed the first time.

Support Sustainable Initiatives: Seek out eco-friendly accommodations, volunteer opportunities, and responsible tour operators on your next return. Continue contributing to Lombok's sustainable future.

Spread the Word: Share your enthusiasm for Lombok with friends and family. Inspire others to travel responsibly and experience the island's unique magic firsthand.

Remember, Lombok's spirit transcends the miles. As you carry its essence within you, know that the island awaits your return, welcoming you with open arms and endless possibilities.

Conclusion

Lombok: A Tapestry Woven with Memories
Lombok, nestled amidst the cerulean expanse of the Indonesian archipelago, is more than just a destination; it's an experience woven into the very fabric of your being. As you turn the final page of this guide, allow yourself to linger in the echoes of sun-kissed days spent lounging on pristine beaches and the thrill of discovering hidden waterfalls nestled within emerald jungles. Remember the warmth of the Lombok people, their smiles etched in your mind like vibrant brushstrokes on a canvas.

This guide has served as your compass, navigating you through Lombok's diverse landscapes and vibrant culture. Yet, the true journey began upon your arrival, with each step forging a path through hidden villages and bustling markets, each sunrise painting the sky anew with possibilities. You've delved into the rich tapestry of history woven into ancient temples and vibrant festivals, feeling the pulse of the island beat beneath your feet.

Beyond the captivating beauty, Lombok whispers of sustainability and responsible travel. It invites you to tread lightly, to leave footprints of respect and appreciation rather than careless impact. Remember the joy of supporting local communities, the thrill of exploring eco-friendly alternatives, and the privilege of witnessing pristine ecosystems thriving. Let your journey be a testament to conscious choices, leaving a legacy of responsible tourism that future generations can inherit.

But Lombok's story isn't confined to these pages. It continues in the quiet whispers of the wind through palm trees, in the rhythm of life unfolding in village squares, and in the laughter of children playing on the shore. Carry these melodies in your heart, allowing them to resurface amidst the mundane of everyday life. Let them remind you of the endless possibilities that await – not just in Lombok, but in every destination you embrace.

This guide may have reached its end, but your Lombok adventure has just begun. As you return to your corner of the world, take with you the spirit of this island paradise. Be a storyteller, sharing its hidden gems and cultural treasures with anyone willing to listen. Be a guardian, advocating for its responsible exploration and sustainable future. And most importantly, be a dreamer, forever chasing the sun-kissed horizons and the vibrant soul of Lombok.

For Lombok is not a place you simply visit; it's a place that seeps into your soul, forever leaving its mark. It's a destination that beckons you back, whispering promises of rediscovery and rejuvenation. And when you answer its call, remember: Lombok awaits, ready to weave new stories and paint memories onto your heart's canvas.

TRAVEL
Journal

DATE: / /

TODAY'S EXPLORATION

TO-DO LIST:

MOOD

☹ 😒 🙁 🙂 😄
ANGRY TIRED SAD HAPPY EXCITED

NOTES/REMINDER:

MEMORIES

Lombok

TRAVEL
Journal

DATE: / /

TODAY'S EXPLORATION

_____
_____
_____
_____
_____
_____
_____
_____

TO-DO LIST:

MOOD

☹ 😑 🙁 🙂 😄
ANGRY TIRED SAD HAPPY EXCITED

NOTES/REMINDER:

MEMORIES

Lombok   89

TRAVEL
Journal

DATE: / /

TODAY'S EXPLORATION

_____
_____
_____
_____
_____
_____
_____
_____
_____

TO-DO LIST:

MOOD

ANGRY   TIRED   SAD   HAPPY   EXCITED

NOTES/REMINDER:

MEMORIES

Lombok

TRAVEL
Journal

DATE: / /

TODAY'S EXPLORATION

TO-DO LIST:

MOOD

☹ 😐 🙁 🙂 😄
ANGRY TIRED SAD HAPPY EXCITED

NOTES/REMINDER:

MEMORIES

Lombok

TRAVEL
Journal

DATE: / /

TODAY'S EXPLORATION

TO-DO LIST:

MOOD

ANGRY   TIRED   SAD   HAPPY   EXCITED

NOTES/REMINDER:

MEMORIES

Lombok

TRAVEL
Journal

DATE: / /

TODAY'S EXPLORATION

_____
_____
_____
_____
_____
_____
_____
_____
_____

TO-DO LIST:

MOOD

☹ 😓 😐 🙂 😆
ANGRY TIRED SAD HAPPY EXCITED

NOTES/REMINDER:

MEMORIES

Lombok

93

TRAVEL
Journal

DATE: / /

TODAY'S EXPLORATION

TO-DO LIST:

MOOD

😟   😐   ☹️   🙂   😃
ANGRY   TIRED   SAD   HAPPY   EXCITED

NOTES/REMINDER:

MEMORIES

Lombok

TRAVEL
Journal

DATE: / /

TODAY'S EXPLORATION
_____
_____
_____
_____
_____
_____
_____
_____
_____
_____

TO-DO LIST:

MOOD

☹ 😐 ☹ 🙂 😄
ANGRY TIRED SAD HAPPY EXCITED

NOTES/REMINDER:
_____
_____
_____
_____

MEMORIES

TRAVEL
Journal

DATE: / /

TODAY'S EXPLORATION

_____
_____
_____
_____
_____
_____
_____
_____

TO-DO LIST:

MOOD

☹ 😐 🙂 😊 😆
ANGRY TIRED SAD HAPPY EXCITED

NOTES/REMINDER:

MEMORIES

Lombok 96

TRAVEL
Journal

DATE: / /

TODAY'S EXPLORATION

TO-DO LIST:

MOOD

ANGRY TIRED SAD HAPPY EXCITED

NOTES/REMINDER:

MEMORIES

Lombok 97

TRAVEL
Journal

DATE: / /

TODAY'S EXPLORATION

_____
_____
_____
_____
_____
_____
_____
_____

TO-DO LIST:

MOOD

😠 😫 🙁 🙂 😄
ANGRY TIRED SAD HAPPY EXCITED

NOTES/REMINDER:

MEMORIES

Lombok

TRAVEL
Journal

DATE: / /

TODAY'S EXPLORATION

_____
_____
_____
_____
_____
_____
_____
_____
_____

TO-DO LIST:

MOOD

😠 😑 🙁 🙂 😃
ANGRY TIRED SAD HAPPY EXCITED

NOTES/REMINDER:

MEMORIES

Lombok 99

TRAVEL
Journal

DATE: / /

TODAY'S EXPLORATION

TO-DO LIST:

MOOD

ANGRY　TIRED　SAD　HAPPY　EXCITED

NOTES/REMINDER:

MEMORIES

Lombok

TRAVEL
Journal

DATE: / /

TODAY'S EXPLORATION
_____
_____
_____
_____
_____
_____
_____
_____

TO-DO LIST:

MOOD
☹ 😐 🙁 🙂 😆
ANGRY TIRED SAD HAPPY EXCITED

NOTES/REMINDER:

MEMORIES

Lombok

TRAVEL
Journal

DATE: / /

TODAY'S EXPLORATION

TO-DO LIST:

MOOD

😠 ANGRY 😫 TIRED 🙁 SAD 🙂 HAPPY 😆 EXCITED

NOTES/REMINDER:

MEMORIES

TRAVEL
Journal

DATE: / /

TODAY'S EXPLORATION

TO-DO LIST:

MOOD

ANGRY　TIRED　SAD　HAPPY　EXCITED

NOTES/REMINDER:

MEMORIES

Lombok

TRAVEL
Journal

DATE: / /

TODAY'S EXPLORATION

TO-DO LIST:

MOOD

😠 ANGRY 😔 TIRED ☹️ SAD 🙂 HAPPY 😄 EXCITED

NOTES/REMINDER:

MEMORIES

Lombok 104

# TRAVEL
Journal

DATE: / /

TODAY'S EXPLORATION

TO-DO LIST:

MOOD

ANGRY TIRED SAD HAPPY EXCITED

NOTES/REMINDER:

MEMORIES

Lombok

TRAVEL
Journal

DATE: / /

TODAY'S EXPLORATION

_____
_____
_____
_____
_____
_____
_____

TO-DO LIST:

_____
_____
_____
_____

MOOD

☹ ANGRY   ☹ TIRED   ☹ SAD   ☺ HAPPY   😄 EXCITED

NOTES/REMINDER:

_____
_____
_____
_____

MEMORIES

_____
_____
_____
_____

Lombok

TRAVEL
Journal

DATE: / /

TODAY'S EXPLORATION

_____
_____
_____
_____
_____
_____
_____
_____

TO-DO LIST:

MOOD

😠 ANGRY 😟 TIRED 🙁 SAD 🙂 HAPPY 😃 EXCITED

NOTES/REMINDER:

MEMORIES

Lombok 107

TRAVEL
Journal

DATE: / /

TODAY'S EXPLORATION

_____
_____
_____
_____
_____
_____
_____

TO-DO LIST:

MOOD

☹ ☹ ☹ ☺ 😀
ANGRY TIRED SAD HAPPY EXCITED

NOTES/REMINDER:

_____
_____
_____
_____

MEMORIES

_____
_____
_____
_____

TRAVEL
Journal

DATE: / /

TODAY'S EXPLORATION

TO-DO LIST:

MOOD

ANGRY TIRED SAD HAPPY EXCITED

NOTES/REMINDER:

MEMORIES

TRAVEL
Journal

DATE: / /

TODAY'S EXPLORATION

TO-DO LIST:

MOOD

😠 😑 🙁 🙂 😆
ANGRY TIRED SAD HAPPY EXCITED

NOTES/REMINDER:

MEMORIES

Lombok 110

TRAVEL
Journal

DATE: / /

TODAY'S EXPLORATION

_____
_____
_____
_____
_____
_____
_____
_____
_____

TO-DO LIST:

MOOD

☹ ☹ ☹ ☺ 😀
ANGRY TIRED SAD HAPPY EXCITED

NOTES/REMINDER:

MEMORIES

TRAVEL
Journal

DATE: / /

TODAY'S EXPLORATION

TO-DO LIST:

MOOD

😠 😒 🙁 🙂 😄
ANGRY TIRED SAD HAPPY EXCITED

NOTES/REMINDER:

MEMORIES

Lombok

TRAVEL Journal

DATE: / /

TODAY'S EXPLORATION

_____
_____
_____
_____
_____
_____
_____
_____

TO-DO LIST:

MOOD

😠 😐 ☹️ 🙂 😄
ANGRY TIRED SAD HAPPY EXCITED

NOTES/REMINDER:

MEMORIES

TRAVEL
Journal

DATE: / /

TODAY'S EXPLORATION
_____
_____
_____
_____
_____
_____
_____
_____
_____

TO-DO LIST:
_____
_____
_____
_____

MOOD

☹ 😐 🙁 🙂 😀
ANGRY TIRED SAD HAPPY EXCITED

NOTES/REMINDER:
_____
_____
_____
_____

MEMORIES
_____
_____
_____
_____

Lombok

TRAVEL
Journal

DATE: / /

TODAY'S EXPLORATION

_____
_____
_____
_____
_____
_____
_____
_____

TO-DO LIST:

MOOD

😠 ANGRY 😒 TIRED 😔 SAD 🙂 HAPPY 😆 EXCITED

NOTES/REMINDER:

MEMORIES

Lombok

TRAVEL
Journal

DATE: / /

TODAY'S EXPLORATION

_____
_____
_____
_____
_____
_____
_____
_____
_____

TO-DO LIST:

MOOD

☹ ANGRY ☹ TIRED ☹ SAD ☺ HAPPY 😃 EXCITED

NOTES/REMINDER:

MEMORIES

Lombok

116

TRAVEL
Journal

DATE: / /

TODAY'S EXPLORATION

_____
_____
_____
_____
_____
_____
_____
_____

TO-DO LIST:

MOOD

☹ 😐 🙁 🙂 😄
ANGRY TIRED SAD HAPPY EXCITED

NOTES/REMINDER:

MEMORIES

Lombok 117

TRAVEL
Journal

DATE: / /

TODAY'S EXPLORATION

TO-DO LIST:

MOOD

☹ 😒 🙁 🙂 😆
ANGRY TIRED SAD HAPPY EXCITED

NOTES/REMINDER:

MEMORIES

Lombok 118

TRAVEL Journal

DATE: / /

TODAY'S EXPLORATION

_____
_____
_____
_____
_____
_____
_____
_____
_____

TO-DO LIST:

MOOD

☹ 😑 🙁 🙂 😁
ANGRY TIRED SAD HAPPY EXCITED

NOTES/REMINDER:

MEMORIES

TRAVEL
Journal

DATE: / /

TODAY'S EXPLORATION

___

TO-DO LIST:

MOOD

☹ 😐 🙁 🙂 😃
ANGRY TIRED SAD HAPPY EXCITED

NOTES/REMINDER:

MEMORIES

Lombok 120

TRAVEL
Journal

DATE: / /

TODAY'S EXPLORATION

TO-DO LIST:

MOOD

ANGRY TIRED SAD HAPPY EXCITED

NOTES/REMINDER:

MEMORIES

Lombok

TRAVEL
Journal

DATE: / /

TODAY'S EXPLORATION

_____
_____
_____
_____
_____
_____
_____
_____

TO-DO LIST:

MOOD

ANGRY   TIRED   SAD   HAPPY   EXCITED

NOTES/REMINDER:

MEMORIES

Lombok

TRAVEL
Journal

DATE: / /

TODAY'S EXPLORATION

TO-DO LIST:

MOOD

☹ 😒 😞 🙂 😆
ANGRY TIRED SAD HAPPY EXCITED

NOTES/REMINDER:

MEMORIES

Lombok

Printed in Great Britain
by Amazon